American Slavery and
the Fight for Freedom

READ
WOKE
BOOKS

THE SLAVE TRADE

BLACK LIVES AND THE DRIVE FOR PROFIT

Elliott Smith

Cicely Lewis, Executive Editor

Lerner Publications ◆ Minneapolis

LETTER FROM CICELY LEWIS

Dear Reader,

Growing up, I learned about Black history only in February. There was a small section in our history textbook about slavery, and then we discussed the Civil Rights Movement. That was it. I always wondered about my ancestors. Did they fight back? How could someone own another human being? What happened between slavery and the Civil Rights Movement?

Then I went to college and took an African American literature class. My whole world opened up as I learned about my history. I started researching and seeking more information. Looking back, I felt like I had been tricked. Why hadn't I learned these things sooner?

Cicely Lewis

As an educator, I want to make sure my students never feel this way. I want you to know:

- Black history didn't begin with slavery.
- Neither Abraham Lincoln nor the Civil Rights Movement ended racism.
- Black people have always fought back.

I want to share the strength, power, *joy*, complexity, and beauty of Black history. This is the gift I hope to give you with this series—but don't stop here. Seek out knowledge wherever you go and question everything.

Yours in solidarity,

—Cicely Lewis, Executive Editor

TABLE OF CONTENTS

Think critically about the photos and illustrations throughout this book. Who is taking the photos or creating the illustrations? What viewpoint do they represent? How does this affect your viewpoint?

The University of South Carolina has two markers on its grounds to recognize the enslaved people who helped build or worked at the college before the Civil War (1861–1865).

SLAVE QUARTERS

This last remaining kitchen and slave quarters on campus stands as a tangible link to the enslaved people who lived and worked here. South Carolina College, forerunner to the modern university, owned a number of slaves and hired countless others between 1801 and 1865. Enslaved people made significant contributions to the construction and maintenance of college buildings and to daily life on campus. Despite limited references to individuals, enslaved workers who appear by name in archival records include Abraham, Amanda, Anna, Anthony, Charles, Henry, Jack, Jim, Joe, Lucy, Mal., Peter, Sancho and his wife, Simon, Toby, and Tom. Naming these individuals is an effort to remember all of those who made significant and substantial contributions to the University of South Carolina.

ERASING HISTORY

RACISM AND PROFIT WERE DRIVING FORCES IN THE GROWTH OF SLAVERY. The transatlantic trade of enslaved people had stops at ports around the southern and eastern coastlines of the US. Hundreds of thousands of enslaved people were brought to these ports during the slave trade.

Many of these places have been stripped of any reference to slavery. There is no mention of what happened there. Only a few markers exist to preserve history and to remember the lives and families affected by auctions and markets.

New Orleans, Louisiana, was the largest port in the slave trade. More than one hundred thousand people were bought and sold there from 1804 to 1862. For years the city wiped away its role in slavery. The only place in the city with a marker was Congo Square, where enslaved people were allowed to gather and dance on Sundays. The city plans to add more markers to show its role in the slave trade and to credit the contributions enslaved people made to New Orleans.

Richmond, Virginia, was the second-largest port of the slave trade. After slavery ended, the city destroyed its slave markets. The city is working to create a memorial park on this sacred ground to recognize the difficult history of the land.

Congo Square marker in New Orleans

On July 28, 2020, Mayor Stoney announces plans to build a memorial park in Shockoe Bottom, which was the center of Richmond's slave trade.

REFLECT

What steps do you think should be taken to remember slave markets?

"Our history in Richmond is good, bad, and ugly," Richmond mayor Levar Stoney said. "And I think we owe it to our ancestors and the descendants of these slaves to tell the complete story, no matter how bad or ugly it might have been."

Places such as the National Museum of African American History and Culture in Washington, DC, help celebrate the lives of Black people and the contributions they have made to America.

Castillo de San Marcos is a national monument in Florida.

CHAPTER 1
WHAT WAS THE SLAVE TRADE?

THE SLAVE TRADE WAS THE CAPTURING OF FREE AFRICANS, BRINGING THEM TO THE AMERICAS, AND SELLING THEM INTO SLAVERY. For more than 350 years, Europeans captured 12.5 million African men, women, and children and sent them on a difficult journey across the Atlantic.

There is no exact date of when the practice started. The Spanish brought enslaved Africans with them as they settled St. Augustine, Florida, in 1565. Records show enslaved people building Castillo de San Marcos, a military fort that is still standing. And many Indigenous peoples were enslaved by English settlers in the Americas. Between 1492 and 1880, an estimated two to five million Indigenous peoples were enslaved in the Americas.

This 1595 engraving by Theodor de Bry shows enslaved Africans working with sugarcane on Hispaniola, an island in the Caribbean.

A painting by Sydney E. King depicts the first Africans arriving in Virginia in 1619.

The year 1619 is an important date in the history of the slave trade in the US. That year, the first enslaved Africans arrived at Point Comfort (present-day Fort Monroe in Hampton) in the English colony of Virginia aboard a ship.

Many countries were involved in selling enslaved people. The Portuguese, Brazilians, French, Dutch, and British were all involved. The British alone captured more than 3.5 million Africans for the long sail to the Americas.

Many African leaders resisted the European trade of enslaved people. Queen Nzinga of Ndongo and Matamba (present-day Angola) fought against the

REFLECT

How do you think greed played a part in the slave trade?

> "In many cases a family was violently divided between three or four enemies, who each led [them] away, to see one another no more."
>
> —Samuel Ajayi Crowther, a former enslaved person who was captured as a teen

Portuguese to prevent the slave trade from expanding into Central Africa.

Before long, private trading companies formed. In the 1600s and 1700s, Britain's Royal African Company and the Dutch West India Company of the Netherlands made massive profits by kidnapping and selling enslaved people. These companies set up a system to ensure the slave trade moved smoothly. Ports like Nantes in France, Rio de Janeiro in Brazil, and Newport, Rhode Island, in the US, became popular stops and economic powers on the backs of the enslaved.

As the US economy began to develop, the need for enslaved people grew. Crops like cotton required hard labor, and enslaved people worked long hours in terrible conditions for no pay. The number of ships headed to US ports continued to grow.

The triangular trade route was used by European merchants who exchanged goods in Africa for enslaved Africans, shipped enslaved Africans to the Americas to sell them, and brought goods from the Americas back to Europe.

CHAPTER 2
THE MIDDLE PASSAGE

BEING CAPTURED WAS JUST THE FIRST EVENT IN THE HORRIBLE FATE FOR MANY ENSLAVED AFRICANS. The next steps proved to be equally difficult.

The triangular trade of slavery was made up of three parts. In the first part, European ships filled with goods such as clothes, guns, and metals left Europe and headed for the western coast of Africa. In Africa the European goods were traded for kidnapped Africans. In the second part, the captured Africans were brought over the Atlantic Ocean to the Americas on ships. In part three, the enslaved Africans were sold in the Americas. After the sale, Europeans bought goods produced from enslaved people's forced labor, like tobacco and sugar, and sailed home to Europe to sell them.

The second part of the triangular trade became known as the Middle Passage. Enslaved Africans mainly spent the monthslong journey packed tightly in the darkness below the ships' decks. Disease spread quickly and easily. Harsh punishments were given to keep the enslaved people in line

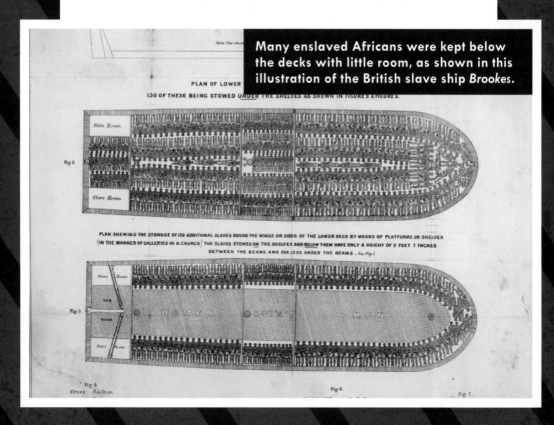

Many enslaved Africans were kept below the decks with little room, as shown in this illustration of the British slave ship *Brookes*.

Olaudah Equiano, also known as Gustavus Vassa, wrote a book about his life as an enslaved person and later took part in the abolitionist movement in Britain.

aboard the ships. An estimated two million people died on the Middle Passage.

One of the most detailed accounts of the Middle Passage comes from Olaudah Equiano. He was taken from Africa and enslaved as a child. He later purchased his freedom and wrote an autobiography.

"The air soon became unfit for breathing, . . . and brought on a sickness among the slaves, of which many died," Equiano wrote of a ship. "This wretched situation was made worse by the chains. The shrieks of women, and the groaning of the dying, created a scene of horror almost unbelievable."

The Zong massacre of 1781 was an example of how terribly enslaved people were treated. On the overcrowded ship, many people began to get sick and some died. The captain ordered his crew to rid those who were ill or dying. In all, 132 people were thrown overboard. Those who were responsible for the enslaved peoples' murders were never held accountable.

THE AMISTAD MUTINY

Many enslaved people tried to change their fate. They often outnumbered crews on ships and revolted. The Amistad mutiny is the most famous. In 1839 Joseph Cinque (*right*) and the other captured Africans on board took control of the *Amistad* as it left Cuba. The ship landed in the US, and the case went to the Supreme Court. The Supreme Court ruled that the men could return to Africa.

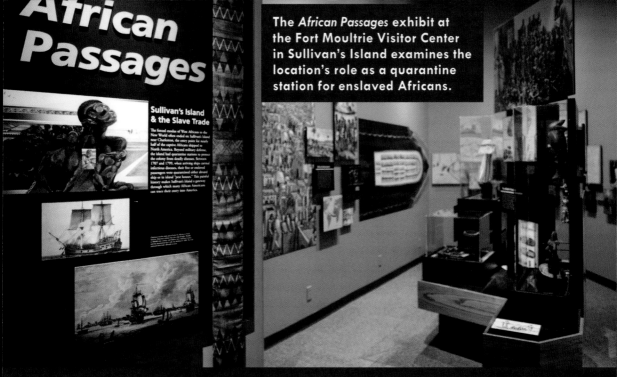

African Passages

The *African Passages* exhibit at the Fort Moultrie Visitor Center in Sullivan's Island examines the location's role as a quarantine station for enslaved Africans.

Sullivan's Island & the Slave Trade

CHAPTER 3
MARKETPLACE

ONCE IN AMERICA, THE SLAVE TRADE TOOK ON A DIFFERENT FORM. Some historians believe tens of thousands of enslaved people found themselves at Sullivan's Island, South Carolina, in the 1700s. The location served as a quarantine station for Africans arriving in the country. Many of them were suffering from deadly diseases that easily spread, such as cholera, smallpox, and measles. The Africans were quarantined on the island before moving on.

After quarantine, enslaved people were brought to pens and jails. Enslaved people would wait there for days or weeks until they were sold to enslavers at auctions. Auctions were regular events in cities across the country. More than 1.2 million people were sold in the US between 1760 and 1860. Auctions were a profitable business. Many white enslavers became wealthy trading Black people.

The auctions were particularly painful for many Black people. These events often tore families apart. Some

10 LIKELY and VALUABLE
SLAVES
AT AUCTION.

On THURSDAY the 24th inst.
WE WILL SELL,

In front of our Office, without any kind of limit or reserve for cash,
AT 11 O'CLOCK,
10 AS LIKELY NEGROES

As any ever offered in this market ; among them is a man who is a superior Cook and House Servant, and a girl about 17 years old, a first rate House Servant, and an excellent seamstress.

Wednesday, July 23, 1823.

An advertisement of an auction of enslaved people in Richmond, Virginia, in 1823

> "Common as are slave-auctions
> in the Southern states, the full
> misery of the event—of the scenes
> which precede and succeed it—is
> never understood till the actual
> experience comes."

—Josiah Henson, a former enslaved person

enslaved people were sold multiple times. This pulled them farther away from any connection to their friends and families.

On March 2 to 3, 1859, the enslaver Pierce Mease Butler held an auction in Georgia. The auction became the largest in US history, with 436 enslaved people sold. Butler made more than $300,000 (more than $9 million today) from the sale.

The event became known as the Weeping Time. The location of the sale was left unrecognized for years. In 2008 the Georgia Historical Society and the City of Savannah placed a marker detailing the auction at a nearby park.

The pens and markets enslaved people were kept in had a new purpose during the Civil War. Many of the

Soldiers stand inside a pen in Alexandria, Virginia, a place where enslaved people were once held after being brought to the Americas.

buildings were used by Union soldiers, people who fought to end slavery in the US, to hold captive Confederate soldiers, people who fought to keep slavery in the US. The Confederate soldiers often complained about the pens' poor conditions.

THE

INJUSTICE AND IMPOLICY

OF THE

SLAVE TRADE,

AND OF THE

Slavery of the Africans:

ILLUSTRATED IN

A SERMON

PREACHED BEFORE THE CONNECTICUT SOCIETY
FOR THE PROMOTION OF FREEDOM, AND FOR
THE RELIEF OF PERSONS UNLAWFULLY HOL-
DEN IN BONDAGE,

AT THEIR ANNUAL MEETING IN NEW-HAVEN,

SEPTEMBER 15, 1791.

CHAPTER 4

STOPPING THE SHIPS

THE TRANSATLANTIC SLAVE TRADE WAS ACTIVE FOR MANY YEARS. But abolitionists wanted to end slavery. Many abolitionists felt slowing the trade would be the first step in ending slavery.

In 1778 Virginia passed a law to stop the importation of enslaved people. Denmark became the first European country to outlaw the slave trade in 1803. Britain followed in 1807, and the US banned the importation of enslaved people in 1808.

Although importing enslaved people became illegal, slavery did not end in the US. It was still legal to trade enslaved people within the country. And Africans continued to be imported illegally into the US for many years after the ban.

Enslaved people were traded throughout the US. Routes were created within the country to help make transporting people easy. And the population of enslaved people continued to grow, even without transporting more

The Foreign Slave Trade Abolition Bill, which prevented the importation of enslaved people by British traders, was passed on March 25, 1807.

kidnapped Africans to the US. Children born of enslaved people were considered the property of enslavers, so children too were enslaved. Many enslavers encouraged or forced enslaved people to have multiple children.

After the slave trade ended, the abolitionist movement declined in the US. It grew again in the 1820s and 1830s. The ban against transatlantic trade did not work exactly as many wanted. But it would mark an important turning point in the fight against slavery.

A family of enslaved people on a plantation in South Carolina in 1862

THE LAST SHIP

In 2019 in southern Alabama's Mobile River, the remains of a ship were discovered. It was the *Clotilda*, the last known (and illegal) ship to enter the US with enslaved people, in 1860. After the Civil War ended, survivors of the *Clotilda* founded Africatown, a small community where many of their descendants live. The discovery of the ship confirms their history. Many are hoping it can be turned into a national monument.

A man visits the Africatown Welcome Center.

PRIMARY SOURCE VOICES

Even after the slave trade ended, the institution of slavery continued in the US for decades. Scan these QR codes to listen to the voices of Black people as they tell their stories of living through slavery. You can also read each speaker's words in the transcript linked below each audio clip.

While you listen, consider the use of the term *slaves*. This book uses the term *enslaved people*. What is the difference between these terms? Also, think about what daily life was like for enslaved people. How were the experiences of enslaved people alike and different from one another?

https://www.loc.gov/item/afc1940003_afs04034a/
Joe McDonald, Livingston, Alabama, 1940

https://www.loc.gov/item/afc1941018_afs05091a/
Isom Moseley, Gee's Bend, Alabama, 1941

This clip mentions "working on shares." This is a reference to sharecropping, an arrangement in which a landowner allows a tenant to use the land in exchange for a share of the crops produced.

https://www.loc.gov/item/afc1984011_afs25659b/
Susan A. Quall, Johns Island, South Carolina,
May 16, 1932

TAKE ACTION

Learning about slavery can help you to understand current racial issues. Here are some ways to educate yourself about the slave trade:

Discover if your city or state has a building that was used in the slave trade. Plan a visit to it with a parent or guardian.

Take a virtual tour of the International Slavery Museum, and learn more about the transatlantic slave trade at https://www.liverpoolmuseums.org.uk /international-slavery-museum/virtual-tour.

Learn more about revolts led by enslaved people that took place on ships or in the US.

Read writings of enslaved people such as Olaudah Equiano to learn about the voyage aboard ships from Africa to America. Browse the pages of Equiano's book *The Interesting Narrative of the Life of Olaudah Equiano, Or Gustavus Vassa, The African* at https://www.loc.gov/resource/rbc0001.2018amimp99422/?st=gallery.

Explore the online collection of slave trade materials from the National Museum of African American History and Culture at https://nmaahc.si.edu/explore/collection/search?edan_local=1&edan_q=slave%2Btrade&.

GLOSSARY

abolitionist: a person who supports ending slavery

auction: a public event where enslaved people were sold to other people

Indigenous: the first people who lived in any region

marker: an item placed at a site to honor the memory of the people who lived there

mutiny: an open rebellion against authorities

port: a town or city with a harbor where ships load or unload cargo

profit: the amount of money earned by a business

quarantine: keeping people, animals, or plants out of a certain area to prevent the spread of disease

revolt: to fight against an authority or government

SOURCE NOTES

6   Casey Cep, "The Fight to Preserve African-American History," *New Yorker*, February 3, 2020, https://www.newyorker.com/magazine/2020/02/03/the-fight-to-preserve-african-american-history.

11   "Personal Stories of Captured Africans," Middle Passage Ceremonies and Port Markers Project (MPCPMP), January 11, 2012, https://www.middlepassageproject.org/2012/01/11/personal-stories-of-captured-africans/?lang=ko.

14   "Olaudah Equiano—Middle Passage Extract 2," Abolition Project, last modified March 12, 2008, http://gallery.nen.gov.uk/audio79020-abolition.html.

18   Anne C. Bailey, "For Hundreds of Years, Enslaved People Were Bought and Sold in America. Today Most of the Sites of This Trade Are Forgotten," *New York Times Magazine*, February 12, 2020, https://www.nytimes.com/interactive/2020/02/12/magazine/1619-project-slave-auction-sites.html#:~:text=%E2%80%9CCommon%20as%20are%20slave%2Dauctions,funded%20by%20the%20Works%20Progress.

READ WOKE READING LIST

Alexander, Richard. *The Transatlantic Slave Trade: The Forced Migration of Africans to America (1607–1830)*. New York: PowerKids, 2016.

Atlantic Slave Trade
https://kids.britannica.com/students/article/Atlantic-slave-trade/602896

Bryan, Ashley. *Freedom over Me: Eleven Slaves, Their Lives and Dreams Brought to Life*. New York: Atheneum Books for Young Readers, 2016.

Lewis, Cicely. *Resistance to Slavery: From Escape to Everyday Rebellion*. Minneapolis: Lerner Publications, 2022.

McKissack, Patricia C. *Amistad: The Story of a Slave Ship*. New York: Random House Books for Young Readers, 2021.

The Middle Passage
https://www.pbs.org/wgbh/aia/part1/1p277.html

Olaudah Equiano
https://www.pbs.org/wgbh/aia/part1/1p276.html

Transatlantic Slave Trade
http://slaveryandremembrance.org/articles/article/?id=A0002

INDEX

PHOTO ACKNOWLEDGMENTS

Image credits: Ken Wolter/Shutterstock.com, p. 4; William A. Morgan/Shutterstock.com, p. 5; AP Photo/Steve Helber, p. 6; Lewis Tse Pui Lung/Shutterstock.com, p. 7; Barbara Smyers/Shutterstock.com, p. 8; Library of Congress, pp. 9, 13, 19, 20; Sydney King/National Park Service, p. 10; Jkwchui/Wikimedia Commons (CC BY-SA 3.0), p. 12; National Museum of African American History, Smithsonian Institution, p. 14; Nathaniel Jocelyn/New Haven Colony Historical Society via Wikipedia Commons, p. 15; Have Camera Will Travel/Alamy Stock Photo, p. 16; Chicago History Museum/Getty Images, p. 17; PA Images/Alamy Stock Photo, p. 21; Everett Collection/Shutterstock.com, p. 22; Jeffrey Greenberg/Universal Images Group/Getty Images; Cecily Lewis portrait photos by Fernando Decillis.

Cover: National Museums Liverpool/Bridgeman Images.

Content consultant credit: Cleopatra Warren, Ph.D., Secondary History Teacher, Atlanta Public Schools, Atlanta, GA

Lerner Publications Company
An imprint of Lerner Publishing Group, Inc.
241 First Avenue North
Minneapolis, MN 55401 USA

For reading levels and more information, look up this title at www.lernerbooks.com.

Main body text set in Aptifer Sans LT Pro.
Typeface provided by Linotype AG.

Editor: Brianna Kaiser **Photo Editor:** Cynthia Zemlicka
Lerner team: Martha Kranes

Library of Congress Cataloging-in-Publication Data

Names: Smith, Elliott, 1976– author.
Title: The slave trade : black lives and the drive for profit / Elliott Smith.
Description: Minneapolis : Lerner Publications, [2022] | Series: American slavery and the fight for freedom (Read woke books) | Includes bibliographical references and index. | Audience: Ages 9–14 | Audience: Grades 4–6 | Summary: "Slavery grew in America with the enslavement of Indigenous peoples and millions of Africans. Learn about the Middle Passage and how the slave trade operated and was brought to its end"— Provided by publisher.
Identifiers: LCCN 2021013750 (print) | LCCN 2021013751 (ebook) | ISBN 9781728439051 (library binding) | ISBN 9781728448206 (paperback) | ISBN 9781728444338 (ebook)
Subjects: LCSH: Slave trade—Africa—History—Juvenile literature. | Slave trade—Atlantic Ocean Region—History—Juvenile literature. | Slavery—United States—History—Juvenile literature.
Classification: LCC HT1322 .S54 2022 (print) | LCC HT1322 (ebook) | DDC 306.3/6209—dc23

LC record available at https://lccn.loc.gov/2021013750
LC ebook record available at https://lccn.loc.gov/2021013751

Manufactured in the United States of America
1-49782-49654-8/17/2021